A MINDFULNESS FOR BEGINNERS JOURNAL

A MINDFULNESS FOR BEGINNERS
JOURNAL

Prompts & Practices for
Living in the Moment

MATTHEW SOCKOLOV

ALTHEA
PRESS

Interior and Cover Designer: Merideth Harte
Photo Art Director/Art Manager: Sara Feinstein
Editor: Emily Angell
Production Editor: Ashley Polikoff
Illustrations © OpiaDesigns / Creative Market, Lana Elanor / Creative Market, Awa Marc / Creative Market, Photohacklovers / Creative Market, Illustration Art Shop / Creative Market

ISBN: 978-1-64152-802-3

CONTENTS

"Stop all of your doingness,
all of your thinking. Just 'be' for a
while. Even for only a moment. It
can change everything."

—NEALE DONALD WALSCH

INTRODUCTION

MINDFULNESS CAME INTO my life when I was a young teenager struggling with behavioral issues and addiction. My father gave me *The Miracle of Mindfulness* by Thich Nhat Hanh. I read the entire book and loved the ideas and practices offered. However, I did not actually put forth the effort to bring mindfulness into my life at that time.

A few years later, as an older teenager, I found myself struggling again. I remembered the idea of mindfulness that my parents had expertly introduced to me. I found a local mindfulness group on the Internet, and, not wanting to go alone, I found a friend to go with me. From that day on, I began a regular sitting meditation practice. The ideas and teachings in the book given to me years ago suddenly became relevant as I was actually practicing mindfulness.

In the years since I began sitting, I have dedicated myself to investigating meditation and mindfulness. I have meditated regularly with various communities in Southern California, spent time on retreat at Buddhist monasteries, and worked one-on-one with mindfulness teachers.

After going through training to teach meditation at Spirit Rock Meditation Center, I opened a meditation center in Northern California. Originally called One Mind Dharma, the center was a donation-based mindfulness center with various classes. My partner, Elizabeth, handled most of the work of running the center while I handled the teaching.

In 2018 we moved to Mexico and into the realm of online mindfulness classes. Today, I teach a free weekly mindfulness class online and work one-on-one with individuals around the world who wish to deepen their mindfulness practice.

I dedicate my life and work to mindfulness because it has impacted me so deeply. I have found relief from many of my worst habits, methods for dealing with anger and anxiety, and techniques for deepening my relationships.

Throughout my years of personal practice, journaling has been an important piece of the puzzle. Although we all learn in different ways, I have found a journal to be one of the greatest tools in investigating mindfulness. With the help of a journal, we can return to our thoughts and experiences in order to recognize patterns, see progress, and learn from past experience. Furthermore, the simple act of writing has the power to help us encode information and insights.

This journal contains prompts, reflections, meditations, practices, quotes, and more. Every activity has a specific flavor to it, but not a specific goal. You will dive into mindfulness practice with each section of the journal, and there is no right or wrong answer. The prompts and reflections simply serve as a jumping-off point for your personal investigation.

Throughout the journal, you will learn how to see your experiences more clearly. Some sections focus on bringing mindfulness to everyday tasks, while others aim to help you work with the anxieties and stresses of life. Think of the journal as a compass, pointing you in the right direction.

It's important to remember that this journal is not a substitute for proper medical care when necessary. It does not take the place of a clinician, therapist, doctor, or medication. This journal can be a powerful asset in your journey, though it is but one instrument in your toolbox.

As you move through the practices and exercises, remember to check in with yourself. Be gentle, give yourself credit for the work you're doing, and keep pushing forward. After leaving a ten-day loving-kindness retreat, I got a tattoo to remind me of a beautiful intention of loving-kindness for myself. You can say these same words to yourself as you work your way through this journal: "I love you; keep going."

Wake Up
to Now

MINDFULNESS BEGINS WITH present-time awareness. We spend most of our days on autopilot, driven by habits and routine. Mindfulness calls for us to turn on the light of awareness and recognize our experience from moment to moment. With practice, you can begin to notice what you are thinking, feeling, doing, and saying.

Mindfulness can help us in many aspects of our lives. Studies have found mindfulness to reduce pain, lower blood pressure, and help the body digest food more effectively. In addition to physical benefits, mindfulness meditation may help us mentally. Recent research suggests mindfulness practice improves overall sleep quality, self-esteem, and working memory. Whether you are working with anxiety or chronic pain, mindfulness is a useful tool to have in your toolbox.

Throughout this journal, you will investigate different avenues to bring yourself to the present moment. The practices and prompts are born from my experience as a meditator, mindfulness teacher, and human. With the guidance of prompts, practices, and quotes, we will uncover ways to focus our attention to the present, return to the present when our minds wander, and find some peace in the ups and downs of daily life.

"The more and more you listen,
the more and more you hear;
the more and more you hear,
the deeper and deeper your
understanding becomes."

—DUDJOM RINPOCHE

What does mindfulness mean to you? Write a few sentences defining mindfulness in your own words.

_____

_____

_____

_____

_____

_____

_____

_____

_____

_____

_____

_____

_____

"Fear is a natural reaction to moving closer to the truth."

—PEMA CHÖDRÖN

Do you have any fears about beginning to practice mindfulness? Do you have doubts about practicing or your abilities? Write your thoughts here.

_____

_____

_____

_____

_____

_____

_____

_____

_____

_____

_____

_____

_____

_____

CALM THE MIND

Close your eyes and bring your attention to the body breathing in the chest. Take a few deep, mindful breaths to help calm the mind and body. Notice the chest expanding as you inhale. Exhale slowly, and imagine letting go of all stress and discomfort. As you let the air go from your lungs, visualize allowing the worry to leave your body. Repeat this practice for as long as you need.

Take a few minutes to think over the last twenty-four hours. Can you identify times in which you were present and times in which you were not? List a few examples of each. Recognize the experiences where you could benefit from being more mindful.

_____

_____

_____

_____

_____

_____

_____

_____

_____

_____

_____

_____

"If you want to conquer the
anxiety of life, live in the
moment, live in the breath."

—AMIT RAY

FOCUS ON YOUR BREATH

Close your eyes for five minutes. Notice where in your body you can feel your breath. You may feel sensations related to breathing in your chest, abdomen, or nostrils. Choose one place in your body to focus your breathing, and simply rest with the experience of breathing. Tune in to the physical sensations of your body breathing here. When the mind wanders off, bring your attention back to this point in your body.

Set a reminder on your phone or computer to pause and practice mindful breathing today. Use the time to take a few deep breaths and return to the present moment. How does it feel to do this during your day? Do you feel any difference before and after you practice mindful breathing? Write about your experience here.

_____

_____

_____

_____

_____

_____

_____

_____

_____

_____

_____

_____

BE PRESENT

———

Today use the practice of awareness triggers, using an everyday event as your reminder to be present. Pick one event or activity you experience regularly, and try to be totally present for it. Feel the sensations in your body, notice your body breathing, listen to the noises around you, and recognize what emotions are present. You may try using the sound of a phone ringing during your day, or the act of brushing your teeth, driving, or anything else you do during your day. Choose one thing, and use it as your time to be fully present and mindful.

When you are experiencing any sort of difficulty, pause to respond with kindness toward yourself. Use the simple phrase "May I be at ease." Think of one simple phrase of kindness you can offer yourself during painful or difficult moments, and write it down here.

_____

_____

_____

_____

_____

_____

_____

_____

_____

_____

_____

_____

Close your eyes, and bring to mind a memory in which you experienced joy. Allow the memory to return, and try to really immerse yourself in the experience. Tune in to what joy feels like. What can you feel in your body? How does the mind feel? Use this space to record these feelings. Bring some curiosity to the experience in order to see it more clearly. Rather than just recognizing it as joy, look at it as if you have never looked at joy before.

_____

_____

_____

_____

_____

_____

_____

_____

_____

_____

_____

OBSERVE YOUR BODY

Find a relaxing position, either sitting or lying down. Without needing to change or fix anything, observe the experience in your body. What sensations can you feel? Do you notice the weight of your clothes on your body, the points of contact where your body is touching the floor or chair, or any pains or aches? Practice mindfulness of the body for five minutes, scanning what sensations and feelings arise.

Sit or lie down in a comfortable position, and allow your eyes to close. Bring your awareness to the crown of your head, tuning in to any sensations you feel here. After a few moments, move to your forehead. Continue moving your awareness slowly through your face, down to your shoulders, and into your arms. Move slowly through your entire body until you reach your toes, focusing your attention on each place as you go. What do you notice in different parts of your body? Describe your experience as you bring awareness to each part of your body.

_____

_____

_____

_____

_____

_____

_____

_____

_____

_____

Consider the movements you make throughout your day. Maybe you walk, type, or drive. Make a list of five different ways you move your body and how each one physically feels. For example, you may use the experience of sitting down. Notice the different muscles moving as you sit, the moment your body makes contact with the chair, and how it feels to rest the body.

1. _____

_____

2. _____

_____

3. _____

_____

4. _____

_____

5. _____

_____

BE IN THE MOMENT

Find a small item of food. Berries work well for this practice, but you can use any food you like. Hold the food in your hand. What do you see? What do you smell? How does it feel in your hand? As you put the food into your mouth, chew slowly. Mindfully observe how it tastes, what textures you notice, and what the experience of eating is like in this moment. Practice being in the moment throughout this exercise.

"Walk as if you are kissing the
Earth with your feet."

—THICH NHAT HANH

Deepen your awareness of your body by practicing a walking meditation. Take a walk around your block or neighborhood, and pay close attention to how you feel. Feel your feet touching the ground, the muscles in your legs engaging, and your entire body moving through space. Describe your experience during this activity.

_____

_____

_____

_____

_____

_____

_____

_____

_____

_____

_____

_____

A MEDITATION FOR LISTENING

Find a comfortable meditation posture and allow your eyes to close for five to ten minutes. Tune in to the experience of hearing. What sounds rise and fall? Notice if a noise is close or far, loud or soft, and pleasant or unpleasant. Investigate each sound that comes into your awareness.

The more we bring mindfulness to our experiences, the more clearly we see and understand how the mind relates to the world. Make a list of experiences you like and ones you dislike. It can be any experience that comes into your mind, from a TV show you like watching to a situation at work that frustrates you. Be honest with yourself and leave the self-judgement behind. As you make your list, consider what each experience feels like in the mind and body. What thoughts, emotions, and feelings enter your mind and body?

LIKE

_____

_____

_____

_____

_____

DISLIKE

_____

_____

_____

_____

_____

LET YOUR BREATH ANCHOR YOU

Allow your eyes to close and take a few deep breaths. During this practice, remember you can always return to your breath to anchor you back to the present moment. Rest in open awareness for ten minutes, allowing your awareness to be free and receiving whatever arises. Mentally note what comes into your awareness. If you hear something, you may note "sound." When the mind begins thinking, note "thinking." If you feel something in the body, use "feeling."

Bring mindfulness to your mental state. Without diving into individual thoughts, check in with your general state of mind in this moment. Is the mind dull or sharp? Is there sleepiness or energy? Are you curious or bored? There is no right or wrong answer. Be true to yourself, and write down what is happening with your mind.

_____

_____

_____

_____

_____

_____

_____

_____

_____

_____

_____

_____

THOUGHTS WILL COME AND GO

Close your eyes for a ten-minute period of mindfulness practice. You can use your breath as your anchor to the present moment, especially when the mind wanders off. Focus your attention on the thinking mind. Observe the thoughts that come to mind and release them, like bubbles floating by. Don't grasp or hold on to any of the thoughts. Just watch them come and go all on their own.

Self-judgement is a pervasive thought pattern. In what ways do you judge yourself harshly or beat yourself up? Are there certain situations where you hold yourself to high or unrealistic standards? Are there pieces of your life that you think should be "better" in some way? Write about the ways self-judgement comes up in your life.

_____

_____

_____

_____

_____

_____

_____

_____

_____

_____

_____

_____

In addition to judging ourselves, we have a tendency to judge others. In what ways do you find yourself judging other people in your life? Are there specific qualities or behaviors in others that irritate you? Make a list of those qualities. This is not to judge yourself or others, but to bring mindfulness to the ways in which our minds interact with the world.

_____

_____

_____

_____

_____

_____

_____

_____

_____

_____

_____

Reflect on what it means to communicate mindfully. What does it look like to speak with mindfulness? Describe what listening with mindfulness means to you. Write about the ways you can begin to communicate more mindfully in your daily life.

_____

_____

_____

_____

_____

_____

_____

_____

_____

_____

_____

_____

AN AFFIRMATION

Affirmations are a powerful tool to help you set clear intentions with your practice. For this affirmation and the affirmations throughout this book, you may repeat the words aloud to yourself, or silently in your head as you go about your day. Try to connect with the words, their meanings, and the overall intention.

I can cultivate a mind that is present and open.

Set aside a few minutes to have a conversation with somebody. You may talk to somebody nearby or pick up the phone and call someone. During your conversation, try to be fully present both in speaking and listening. You may let the person know you are practicing mindfulness, or just have a normal conversation. Write about what you noticed, what you found difficult, if your mind wandered, and how this practice may benefit you going forward.

_____

_____

_____

_____

_____

_____

_____

_____

_____

_____

_____

_____

"Much of spiritual life is
self-acceptance; maybe all of it."

—JACK KORNFIELD

Where in your life do you find self-acceptance to be difficult? Are there situations you experience or qualities in yourself that you struggle to accept? Bring your awareness to these difficulties and write them down.

As you have started to investigate being present, you have likely experienced difficulties with mindfulness. What makes it hard to be present? Are there events during your day that take you out of the moment? When you sit in meditation practice, what pulls your mind away? Write a list of the most common things that pull your mind away from meditation.

_____

_____

_____

_____

_____

_____

_____

_____

_____

_____

_____

A LOVING-KINDNESS MEDITATION

Close your eyes and take a few deep breaths to settle. Offer a few phrases of loving-kindness silently
to yourself, cultivating an intention of friendliness
toward your body, mind, and heart. Use the phrases:
"May my body be at ease," "May my mind be at ease," and
"May my heart be at ease." Repeat these phrases in your
head, connecting with your intention to be kind to these
different parts of your experience.

"While meditating we are simply seeing what the mind has been doing all along."

—ALLAN LOKOS

During the day, you may find yourself falling out of mindfulness and into autopilot mode. There are mundane tasks we do without thinking, such as making our morning coffee, responding to e-mails, or paying our bills. Where do you fall into autopilot in your life? Think about the last few days for ideas and insight, and make a list of your autopilot moments.

_____

_____

_____

_____

_____

_____

_____

_____

_____

_____

_____

_____

Let Thoughts Flow Through You

WHEN YOU BEGIN bringing more attention to your experience, you are likely to come into contact with difficult thoughts and emotions. They come up seemingly out of nowhere and hook you in. We have moments of anger, flashes of anxiety, or hours where a thought won't leave us alone. These experiences may be why you came to meditation practice, and the good news is that mindfulness gives us an opportunity to work through them.

Mindful or not, these thoughts and emotions are happening now. The practice of mindfulness is not to stop these experiences, but to change our relationships with them. This starts with simple awareness. We can best serve ourselves by tuning in to the difficulties and observing with curiosity, rather than resistance.

One of the qualities we can recognize is that these emotions and thoughts are impermanent. Even when they linger, they do not stay forever. They ebb and flow. The following prompts and practices will encourage you to relate to your thoughts in a new way. Rather than being entangled with experiences, good and bad, we will be able to observe them floating by, like clouds in the sky.

"Let everything happen to you:
beauty and terror. Just keep
going. No feeling is final."

—RAINER MARIA RILKE

COME BACK TO YOUR BREATH

Find a comfortable posture for a period of meditation. Bring your attention to the sensation of your breath in your body. When something else grabs your attention, practice coming back to your breath. Recognize your innate ability to leave a thought or emotion and return to the present-time experience in your body.

"Impermanence is a principle of harmony. When we don't struggle against it, we are in harmony with reality."

—PEMA CHÖDRÖN

Thoughts and emotions are constantly changing. Through the practice of mindfulness, we can see the impermanent nature of our experience. Describe how you experience impermanence and change in your life. Are there specific emotions or thoughts that come and go? Do you go through times where your thoughts bounce from one thing to the next and you can't seem to focus?

_____

_____

_____

_____

_____

_____

_____

_____

_____

_____

Although pain and difficulties arise in many forms, people generally have certain painful situations and emotions that seem to come up frequently. Encourage mindfulness by reflecting on what difficulties you struggle with most often. Are there specific thoughts or emotions that seem to knock you off balance? Do certain people or situations rub you the wrong way? Make a list of the difficulties you struggle with most.

_____

_____

_____

_____

_____

_____

_____

_____

_____

_____

With a mindfulness practice, we learn to respond with wisdom and calm instead of with impatience and anger. However, we have to begin by recognizing the places where we become reactive. What occurrences in your life do you find yourself reacting to without thinking? Describe the moments where you lapse out of mindfulness and fall into reactivity.

_____

_____

_____

_____

_____

_____

_____

_____

_____

_____

_____

_____

Find a comfortable sitting position and close your eyes. Connect with your own desire to be happy and at peace. With the intention of cultivating loving-kindness for yourself, begin repeating some phrases silently in your head. You can use the phrases "May I be happy," "May I be healthy," "May I be safe," and "May I be at ease." Continue to repeat these phrases in your mind for ten minutes. When you have finished, write down your favorite phrase so that you can refer back to it.

_____

_____

_____

_____

_____

_____

_____

_____

_____

_____

Tuning in to the impermanence of thoughts and emotions can help us let go of those that are difficult. In this moment, open your awareness to the experience of hearing. Can you hear the rise and fall of sounds? Notice the moment a noise approaches, and when you can no longer hear it. Describe the sounds that are coming and going.

_____

_____

_____

_____

_____

_____

_____

_____

_____

_____

TUNE IN TO YOUR BODY

For this practice, you can sit or lie down. Tune in to the physical sensations of your body. When a sensation comes into your awareness, try to recognize the impermanent nature of it. Can you feel the sensation changing, moving, or subsiding? Allow your attention to move to other sensations in your body and continue to be attuned to the changes you experience.

Bring to mind a mental or emotional difficulty you experience. Part of this obstacle is a mental state or pattern of thinking. Write down what this difficulty feels like in the mind. What thoughts come up? Do anxiety, dullness, irritation, or any other overall mental state arise?

———————————————————————————

———————————————————————————

———————————————————————————

———————————————————————————

———————————————————————————

———————————————————————————

———————————————————————————

———————————————————————————

———————————————————————————

———————————————————————————

———————————————————————————

AN AFFIRMATION

---

*I give myself permission to feel
my emotions today.*

Stay with the same difficulty in your mind. Rather than focusing on the mental aspect, pay attention to what is happening in your body. Does your breath change when you recall this difficulty? Do any muscles tense? Does your body feel calm or agitated? Write about your personal experience in your body with this challenging emotion or thought.

_____

_____

_____

_____

_____

_____

_____

_____

_____

_____

_____

_____

"Being mindful means that we suspend judgment for a time, set aside our immediate goals for the future, and take in the present moment as it is rather than as we would like it to be."

—J. MARK G. WILLIAMS

You have begun to investigate the places where you are reactive rather than responsive. With this difficulty you have been exploring, what would be a wise response? Write it down. How can you meet the obstacle with compassion and clear-headedness? You may also consider an unwise response in order to get a clearer picture of what may be useful and healthy.

_____

_____

_____

_____

_____

_____

_____

_____

_____

_____

_____

_____

A MEDITATION FOR SELF-COMPASSION

Settle into a comfortable position and allow your eyes to close. Bring to mind the difficulty you're experiencing. Instead of attempting to fix the problem or push it away, try to respond with compassionate care. Offer yourself some phrases of sympathy silently in your head, such as "May I be free from this pain," "May I care about this difficulty," and "May I have compassion."

Compassion meditation can help train us to respond with care when life becomes difficult. Today, notice when you are struggling with something. Take a moment to put your hand over your heart and offer yourself a few phrases of compassion. Reflect and record how this changes your experience of the obstacle.

_____

_____

_____

_____

_____

_____

_____

_____

_____

_____

_____

_____

RELEASE YOUR STRUGGLES

There are many ways to express emotions and thoughts. Use the space below to doodle or draw something with which you struggle. Allow yourself the freedom to create whatever comes to mind, whether it is a depiction of something real or an abstract piece.

Bring a difficult emotion or pattern of thinking to your mind. Examples may be self-judgement, anxiety, or anger. In an effort to change your relationship to it, give it a playful name. I often find myself gripped by fear, so I named my fear "Courage," after the cartoon *Courage the Cowardly Dog*. Write about the name you gave your emotion and why you chose it.

_____

_____

_____

_____

_____

_____

_____

_____

_____

_____

_____

_____

Make a list of five things that cause you stress. You do not need to fix any of them right now, and there is no need to beat yourself up. Simply make a list, acknowledging these experiences and bringing them into your awareness.

1. the kid's school

2. ~~trying~~ to manage my work load)

3. Cooking (want everything to come out right)

4. House (just want to be done decorating)

5. Letters for the kids (need to write more)

How does each stressor on your list impact your life? When you are stressed, how does your life look different? Do you eat differently? How are your relationships in moments of stress? Does your energy level change? Bring mindfulness to the effects of stress in your life by beginning to identify its presence and how it impacts you.

(1) the only stressors that affect my life are 1 & 2 They definately cause me to eat differently but my life doesn't look different, but they do make me tired.

Create a list of emotions you have felt over the past week. No emotion is too small. From fear and sadness to joy and gratitude, include it all. When you think you are done, keep digging deeper and write down all the emotions you find within yourself.

_____

_____

_____

_____

_____

_____

_____

_____

_____

_____

_____

A MEDITATION FOR
SORTING THROUGH EMOTIONS

You can keep your eyes open during this meditation period so you can look at your list of emotions. Begin with the first emotion on your list and bring it to mind. What does it feel like in your mind and body? Continue through your list, being mindful of each emotion in order to understand it more clearly and deeply.

RESPOND WITH WISDOM

Mindfulness begins with acknowledging the emotions that surface, but we are also called to respond with wisdom. With each of the emotions on your list, reflect on what a wise response may be. You may appreciate joy, have compassion for anxiety, etc. For example, if joy arises, you may respond with gratitude. If you experience anxiety, the wise response may be self-compassion.

TAP IN TO YOUR EMOTIONS

Without blaming yourself, consider what may cause or influence the emotions on your list to arise. Is there something you do (or don't do) that makes the emotion more likely to surface? Be mindful of the whole process of the emotion, from the causes and influences of the emotion itself to the emotion subsiding.

What can you do to discourage the unpleasant emotions and encourage the pleasant ones? Are there any habits or actions that may be conducive to creating happiness? You cannot guarantee an emotion will or will not arise, but you can take action. Make a list of what is within your power to change.

_____

_____

_____

_____

_____

_____

_____

_____

_____

_____

_____

_____

"If you let go a little, you will have a little peace. If you let go a lot, you will have a lot of peace. If you let go completely, you will have complete peace."

—AJAHN CHAH

Some things are not within your control. Recognizing this can help us accept, rather than resist, our reality. Make a list of at least three things you don't have control over, paying special attention to the ones you have difficulty letting go.

1. _____

2. _____

3. _____

4. _____

5. _____

A MEDITATION TO RELEASE CONTROL

Let your body settle into a comfortable position, and allow your eyes to close for ten minutes of meditation. Bring to mind some of the items from your list of things you have no control over. In an effort to let go, use the simple phrase "I am not in control of _____." Continue with different items on your list, recognizing where it is difficult to let go.

Make a gratitude list. Let anything for which you're grateful make it onto the page. It may be a being, an experience, a place, or anything else that comes up for you. As you make your list, tune in to the experience of appreciation with each item.

_____

_____

_____

_____

_____

_____

_____

_____

_____

_____

_____

_____

EMBRACE THE PRESENT

The British monk Ajahn Sumedho uses the mantra "Right now, it's like this." Use this mantra during your day to encourage mindfulness. Recognize that what is happening is what is happening, and use these words to remind yourself that you don't need to change or fix it. Just be present with how it is.

Live in the Moment

THE MIND'S JOB is to process information. It thinks, solves problems, analyzes, worries, and gets bored. When our attention wanders off or we fall back into autopilot, we do not need to criticize ourselves. It is just the mind doing its job. With proper training, we can break these habits and cultivate an ability to return to the present moment.

Imagine the mind is a muscle and mindfulness is your barbell. In order to strengthen your muscle, you have to use your barbell. Like going to the gym, you must repeat an action in order to experience growth. When the mind wanders off, we are presented with an opportunity to lift that barbell and bring our attention back to the present moment. Every time we do so, we are strengthening that mental muscle.

This section will focus on bringing the mind back to the present moment. We will learn to treat the wandering mind as an opportunity, not a problem. By remembering the mind is just doing its job, you can let go of self-judgement. With some kindness and patience, you can change your relationship to your restless mind.

"That's life: starting over,
one breath at a time."

—SHARON SALZBERG

When does mindfulness come most naturally to you? What time of the day are you naturally present? When do you find it most difficult to live in the present? Record your findings.

_____

_____

_____

_____

_____

_____

_____

_____

_____

_____

_____

_____

_____

_____

_____

Write down your daily routine. What activities do you take part in regularly? This may include brushing your teeth, getting dressed, eating, driving, answering e-mails, talking to your kids, etc. Rather than allowing yourself to go into autopilot or grow anxious, consider how you can bring some mindfulness and ease to each action.

Sit in a comfortable position and close your eyes. Keep your journal nearby. You can bring your attention to your breath as your anchor to the present moment. When your mind wanders off, open your eyes and write a word or phrase that describes where it wandered. Begin to really tune in to what your mind is doing.

_____

_____

_____

_____

_____

_____

_____

_____

_____

_____

_____

"Every time we become
aware of a thought, as opposed
to being lost in a thought,
we experience that opening
of the mind."

—JOSEPH GOLDSTEIN

Two integral parts of mindfulness are non-judgement and nonattachment. Are there specific thoughts or emotions where you find yourself lost, attached, or judgmental? Describe these thoughts or emotions.

As hard as you may try to concentrate, the mind will naturally wander at times. Part of the reason this happens is that the mind can have non-volitional thoughts. That is, the mind thinks thoughts without our input or control. What are some thoughts that arise for you without you wanting them to? Compile a list of those thoughts here.

Whether we are experiencing anxiety or anger or just off wandering in a fantasy, the mind sometimes does not do what we want. How we respond in these moments has the power to deeply influence our relationship with the mind. Write down how you respond when the mind does not cooperate. What is a skillful response?

_____

_____

_____

_____

_____

_____

_____

_____

_____

_____

_____

_____

TAKE A MINDFUL WALK

Investigate mindfulness while walking. Set aside some time to take a walk, in nature if you are able. Just walk and be present. Listen to the noises, see the sights, feel the body walking, and smell the smell of nature. When the mind wanders, gently bring it back to your walk.

A SIMPLE CUP OF TEA

The mundane tasks we complete during our days are often the times when our mind wanders. We don't need much brainpower to make a cup of tea or coffee, so the mind has free resources to stroll. Make yourself a cup of coffee or tea, and try to be present with each step of the experience. When thoughts arise, acknowledge them, and come back to your task.

AN AFFIRMATION

Breathing in, I calm the body.
Breathing out, I let go of stress.

During your day, bring some attention to multitasking. You can encourage your mind to be focused and mindful by engaging in just one task at a time. Make a list of the times when you find yourself multitasking. Describe what it feels like to let go of something you are doing and just handle one thing at a time.

"Let your body relax and your heart soften. Open to whatever you experience without fighting. Let go of the battle. Breathe quietly and let it be."

—JACK KORNFIELD

What experiences do you fight in your life? Describe the emotions or thoughts that you resist instead of leaving them be. Where can you let your heart soften and open?

When the mind jumps around from one thing to the next, we call it a "monkey mind." Like a monkey swinging from tree to tree, the mind sometimes won't settle. It constantly looks for the next thing. Where and when do you experience monkey mind in your life? Write down some signs you recognize when your mind is doing this.

Sometimes, you may notice that the mind wanders for self-analysis. Describe the ways your mind falls into the habit of analyzing yourself. Do you compare yourself to others? Do you think about where you "should" be or what your practice "should" feel like? Write down whether you feel these thoughts are true and useful.

_____

_____

_____

_____

_____

_____

_____

_____

_____

_____

_____

_____

LET THOUGHTS COME AND GO

Prepare for a meditation period of about ten minutes. Bring your attention to the experience of your body breathing. Whenever a thought comes up, don't engage with it. Simply allow it to pass by in the background while you stay with the experience of each inhalation and exhalation. What does it feel like to allow thoughts to come and go without engaging?

Thinking of the mind as a muscle, are there other ways you can train it? When a mental muscle is strong, we are no longer as susceptible to mind-wandering. How can you strengthen your mind's ability to focus during your daily life? Do you multitask frequently, check social media during the day, or talk on the phone while writing e-mails? Are you listening to music or the radio while driving? Make a list of three ways you can minimize distraction and stay on track.

1. _____

2. _____

3. _____

The wandering mind can become especially active when certain mental states arise. When you find your mind wandering in meditation or daily life, what is your mental state? Is your mind bored? Is it sleepy and losing sharpness? Is it anxious and energized? Write down your thoughts.

Take a short walk. As you do, practice mindfulness by observing your mind. Allow it to wander freely. Whatever thought, emotion, sound, smell, or sight comes up, just observe. Can you be mindful and clearly see the thoughts? Can you watch your experience bounce around without resistance? Write about your experience observing the mind.

Bring mindfulness to the experience of seeing. What can you see in this moment? Make a list of items, colors, shapes, material, textures, movement, and anything else you notice in your environment.

_____

_____

_____

_____

_____

_____

_____

_____

_____

_____

_____

_____

_____

_____

PREPARE A MINDFUL MEAL

Cook yourself a meal. From the shopping and preparation all the way through the eating, be completely present and mindful. Tune in to the experience from start to finish, and notice when the mind begins to wander off.

Where does your mind go most often when it wanders? Does it plan? Maybe it analyzes. Does it fall into regret or rethinking a conversation? Write down the major ways in which your mind wanders.

_____

_____

_____

_____

_____

_____

_____

_____

_____

_____

_____

_____

_____

_____

We can benefit from holding ourselves to certain standards. However, the harsh self-criticizing voice we have is not useful. If you allow space for the criticizing voice, what does it say? Are there specific qualities or behaviors you're especially critical of? Ask yourself, if there is truth to this criticism, what is the kindest way you can respond to it? Record how you would respond to yourself.

Instead of engaging with your critical voice, meet it with a louder affirmative voice. Write a few phrases or affirmations you can offer yourself when you notice the critical voice surfacing. For example, you may use the phrase "I am right where I am supposed to be in this moment."

BE KIND TO YOURSELF

Close your eyes and take a few deep breaths with the intention of directing kindness toward yourself. Recognizing that you have the ability to change your relationship with your mind, bring up an intention of friendliness and gentleness toward it. In your head, repeat the two simple phrases "May my mind be at ease" and "May I be at ease with my mind." Continue with these phrases for ten minutes.

Other than loving-kindness meditations, how can you encourage a kind and gentle relationship with your mind? Can you make an effort to work with certain patterns of thought? Are there healthier decisions you could make in your life to encourage more patience? Write a few ways you can encourage self-kindness.

_____

_____

_____

_____

_____

_____

_____

_____

_____

_____

_____

_____

AN AFFIRMATION

May I both love and be loved.
I deserve both.

"If you're not hearing
mindfulness in some deep
way as heartfulness, you're not
really understanding it."

—JON KABAT-ZINN

How can you bring more kindness to your mindfulness practice? How can you respond to your mind with gentleness and patience, especially when it isn't doing what you want it to? Describe methods for both meditation periods and daily life.

Create a few of your own personal affirmations and phrases. Write one affirmation with the intention of recognizing your potential to change. For example, "I am capable of change." For the second, encourage kindness and gentleness toward your mind, such as "May I make friends with my mind." Finally, create one to inspire mindfulness, such as "May I be here now." Offer these affirmations to yourself in the mirror today.

"In this moment, there is plenty of time. In this moment, you are precisely as you should be. In this moment, there is infinite possibility."

—VICTORIA MORAN

Savor the Present

WITH A MINDFULNESS practice, it is important to remember that it is indeed a practice. Continuing to dedicate time and energy to being aware will reward you with more moments of mindfulness throughout your day. However, we may find our commitment to mindfulness coming and going. We may go days or weeks without stopping to savor a truly present moment.

Through reinforcing habits, identifying weaknesses, and continuing to check in with yourself, you can discover how to build a sustainable and lasting mindfulness practice. What works for you may be different from what works for the next person. We can benefit from being open to experimenting with new ideas and practices in order to find what suits our individual lifestyles.

In this final section, we look closely at our relationship to mindfulness. You have resources, both internal and external, to support and encourage your mindfulness practice. The guidance here encourages you to lay a foundation of mindfulness that carries you forward and helps you continue the growth you have started.

"To earn the trust of your meditation, you have to visit it every day. It's like having a puppy."

—CHELSEA RICHER

Write yourself a letter about how mindfulness is impacting your life. Include the positives and the negatives of your mindfulness practice. What do you feel you are gaining from mindfulness? What do you feel you are struggling with from mindfulness?

_____

_____

_____

_____

_____

_____

_____

_____

_____

_____

_____

_____

As you continue to cultivate mindfulness, what are your goals? How do you want mindfulness to help you grow and change? What do you hope to gain out of a consistent mindfulness practice? List at least three goals on this page.

1.

2.

3.

AN AFFIRMATION

I contain within me the seeds of mindfulness, joy, compassion, patience, and calm.

"Listen to your heart and trust the direction you're being pulled. Something inside you already knows what to do."

—SPRING WASHAM

You've recognized your goals with mindfulness practice; now what can you do to realize them? What is required for you to reach your goals? Write your thoughts below.

ESTABLISH A REGULAR PRACTICE

Make a resolution to sit in meditation regularly for a set period of time. Commit to meditating for five or ten minutes a day. You may work with your breath, phrases of loving-kindness, or any other practice you've found in this journal. You may also look in the Resources section at the end of this book (page 142) for information on where to find guided meditations.

Make a gratitude list of qualities and behaviors you see in yourself when you are mindful and at ease. How has mindfulness helped you grow? Describe what you have gained here.

Make a list of actions you can take to help cultivate a habit of mindfulness meditation. Can you sit in the same location in your home every day? Perhaps you are also able to sit at the same time every day. Do you enjoy sitting with a candle or a cup of tea? Write down other ideas so you can encourage yourself to create a mindfulness routine.

BUILD A ROUTINE

Look over some of the habits and actions you listed in the previous reflection, and begin to implement them. Sit in meditation for ten minutes in the same location or at the same time every day for one week. Begin to build a routine to encourage your mindfulness practice to continue. What works, and what does not?

"In today's rush, we all think too much, seek too much, want too much and forget about the joy of just being."

—ECKHART TOLLE

HOW CAN YOU CHANGE AND GROW?

Reflect upon your growing edges, those places where you have room to grow. Are there weak spots in your mindfulness practice, or places where you struggle? Without judgement, sit in silence for several minutes and recognize the ways in which you struggle to be present.

Curiosity can be a powerful fuel for mindfulness practice. Write down a few things you would like to better understand and see clearly about yourself. Are there specific emotions, thoughts, or experiences you would like to be more mindful of? Where does curiosity emerge naturally?

Tune in to all of your sense doors, the senses of sight, smell, taste, hearing, feeling, and thinking. Write down five things you can see right now, four things you can feel in the body, three things you can hear, two things you smell, and one thing you can taste. Also make note of anything you are thinking and feeling.

SELF-CHECK

Close your eyes for a short period of meditation. You may start with a minute of focusing on your breath. Ask yourself, how am I doing right now? Is there anything on your mind? Check in with yourself. If you become overwhelmed by your thoughts, bring your focus back to your breath.

One way to encourage mindfulness practice is to have support. Is there anyone else in your life with whom you could practice or whom you could ask questions about their practice? Make a list of people who may be interested in mindfulness or already have a mindfulness-based practice.

"Every morning we are born again. What we do today is what matters most."

—JACK KORNFIELD

Identify and write down one time you can be mindful in the morning, the afternoon, and the evening. For example, you may choose getting dressed in the morning, eating lunch, and lying down in bed at night. How do these moments throughout your day encourage mindfulness all day long?

Put forth effort to be mindful of the start and end of your day. Bring awareness to the experience of getting ready for bed. Describe your routine. In the morning, see how soon you can be present upon waking. What is the first breath you are mindful of during your day?

_____

_____

_____

_____

_____

_____

_____

_____

_____

_____

_____

_____

_____

What does it feel like to be mindful and present? Describe how you know when you are present and when you are not.

_____

_____

_____

_____

_____

_____

_____

_____

_____

_____

_____

_____

_____

_____

"You can wait for a miracle,
but it's generally a better
strategy to meet it halfway."

—ROBERT BRAULT

Growth, peace, and freedom from stress won't arise out of nowhere. It takes effort and dedication. List five ways you can continue to encourage yourself on this path.

1. _____

2. _____

3. _____

4. _____

5. _____

Investigate the principle of effort in your life. Where do you overexert yourself and become exhausted? Where do you put forth minimal effort? What does it feel like to put forth the perfect amount of effort? Bring mindfulness to the effort in your life, and write about where you put too much or too little.

Prepare for the times in which you lack energy in your mindfulness practice. What can you do when you don't feel like meditating, or when you lose steam with your practice? Come up with a simple and actionable plan, and write it out.

Patience is a key aspect of the path of mindfulness. Create a personal mantra to use when you grow impatient with your growth and practice. Use a simple phrase, such as "No need to rush," or "May I be patient with myself."

AN AFFIRMATION

My mind is capable, my body is resilient, and my heart is full.

"If you want others to be happy, practice compassion. If you want to be happy, practice compassion."

HAVE COMPASSION FOR OTHERS

Recognize when somebody is going through difficulty. Even if it is minor, try to open your heart and have compassion. Where do you see people struggling in your life? How can you help them through a mindful practice?

MOVE THROUGH THE
WORLD WITH KINDNESS

Bring mindfulness and kindness to your interactions with others. When you see other people, offer a silent phrase of loving-kindness in your head. Whether you're driving, walking down the street, or at work, offer the simple phrase "May you be at ease." How does this change your experience of moving through the world?

What internal resources can you utilize to continue your mindfulness practice? Recognize and make a list of your strengths and how these qualities can help support your practice.

What external resources do you plan on using to continue your practice? Do you prefer to read books or listen to audiobooks? Can you find podcasts, mobile apps, or guided meditations? Are there meditation groups nearby, or do you have a mindfulness buddy? Make a plan, and write it below. (You can incorporate books, apps, podcasts, and centers from the Resources section on page 142).

We sometimes forget to pause and appreciate ourselves. As we come to the end of this journal experience—and the continuation of your mindfulness practice—give yourself credit for achievements in self-reflection. Make a list of things you appreciate specifically about yourself. Are there qualities, characteristics, or behaviors you appreciate for some reason? Why do you appreciate each one?

CHERISH YOURSELF

Take the list you just created, and go through each item one at a time. You can close your eyes, if you'd like. Tune in to how it feels to recognize and mindfully appreciate yourself. Can you tune in to the joy, ease, or gratitude? What does it feel like to appreciate yourself and your life? How can you set aside time in your continuing practice to remember to pause and cherish yourself?

"Have patience with all things,
But, first of all with yourself."

—SAINT FRANCIS DE SALES

RESOURCES

BOOKS

Breath by Breath: The Liberating Practice of Insight Meditation by David Guy and Larry Rosenberg

Buddha's Brain: The Practical Neuroscience of Happiness, Love, and Wisdom by Rick Hanson

A Burning Desire: Dharma God and the Path of Recovery by Kevin Griffin

A Fierce Heart: Finding Strength, Courage, and Wisdom in Any Moment by Spring Washam

The Miracle of Mindfulness: An Introduction to the Practice of Meditation by Thich Nhat Hanh

A Path with Heart: A Guide Through the Perils and Promises of Spiritual Life by Jack Kornfield

Radical Acceptance: Embracing Your Life with the Heart of a Buddha by Tara Brach

Real Happiness: The Power of Meditation: A 28-Day Program by Sharon Salzberg

WEBSITES AND MAGAZINES

Access to Insight: www.accesstoinsight.org

Greater Good Magazine: greatergood.berkeley.edu

Mindful: www.mindful.org

Mindful Schools: www.mindfulschools.org

Dr. Kristen Neff: www.self-compassion.org

Tricycle: www.tricycle.org

Wildmind: www.wildmind.org

MOBILE APPS

Insight Timer: www.insighttimer.com

Calm: www.calm.com

Headspace: www.headspace.com

MetaFi: www.metafi.me

Ten Percent Happier: www.tenpercent.com

PODCASTS AND TALKS

Audio Dharma: www.audiodharma.org

Tara Brach: www.tarabrach.com/talks-audio-video

Buddhist Geeks: podcast.buddhistgeeks.org

Dharma Seed: www.dharmaseed.org/talks

Metta Hour Podcast: www.sharonsalzberg.com
    /metta-hour-podcast

Ten Percent Happier Podcast with Dan Harris: www.tenpercent
    .com/podcast

The Science of Happiness: greatergood.berkeley.edu/podcasts

The Secular Buddhist Podcast: www.secularbuddhism.org
    /category/podcasts

MEDITATION CENTERS

East Bay Meditation Center: www.eastbaymeditation.org

Insight Meditation Center: www.insightmeditationcenter.org

Insight Meditation Community of Washington: www.imcw.org

Insight Meditation Society: www.dharma.org

InsightLA: www.insightla.org

Spirit Rock: www.spiritrock.org

Vipassana Meditation: www.dhamma.org

REFERENCES

Brault, Robert. *Round up the Usual Suspects: Thoughts on Just about Everything*. Createspace Independent Publishing, 2014.

Chah, Ajahn. *Food for the Heart: The Collected Teachings of Ajahn Chah*. Somerville: Wisdom Publications, 2002.

Chödrön, Pema. *When Things Fall Apart: Heart Advice for Difficult Times*. London: Thorsons Classics, 2017.

Dalai Lama, His Holiness the, Howard C. Cutler, M.D. *The Art of Happiness*. New York: Riverhead Books, 1998.

David Lynch Foundation. "Film Student Chelsea Richer on Creativity and Meditation." YouTube. October 17, 2012. Accessed May 24, 2019. https://www.youtube.com/watch?v=O2X8DY5fWBw.

Goldstein, Joseph. *Insight Meditation: The Practice of Freedom*. Boston: Shambhala, 2003.

Hanh, Thich Nhat. *Peace Is Every Step: The Path of Mindfulness in Everyday Life*. Edited by Arnold Kotler. London: Bantam Books, 1992.

Kabat-Zinn, Jon. *Wherever You Go, There You Are: Mindfulness Meditation in Everyday Life*. New York: Hachette Books, 2005.

Kornfield, Jack. *Buddha's Little Instruction Book*. New York: Bantam Books, 1994.

Kornfield, Jack. *A Path with Heart: A Guide Through the Perils and Promises of Spiritual Life*. New York: Bantam Books, 2002.

Lokos, Allan. *Patience: The Art of Peaceful Living*. New York: TarcherPerigee, 2012.

Moran, Victoria. *Younger by the Day: 365 Ways to Rejuvenate Your Body and Revitalize Your Spirit*. San Francisco: HarperOne, 2004.

Ray, Amit. *OM Chanting and Meditation*. Lexington, KY: Inner Light Publishers, 2010.

Rilke, Rainer Maria. *Letters to a Young Poet*. Translated by Stephen Mitchell. New York: Modern Library, 2001.

Rinpoche, Dudjom. *Counsels from My Heart*. New Delhi: Shechen Publications, 2004.

Salzberg, Sharon. *Lovingkindness: The Revolutionary Art of Happiness*. Boulder: Shambhala, 2002.

Tolle, Eckhart. *The Power of Now: A Guide to Spiritual Enlightenment*. Vancouver: Namaste Publishing, 2007.

Walsch, Neale Donald. *Conversations with God: An Uncommon Dialogue, Book 1*. New York: G.P. Putnam's Sons, 2019.

Washam, Spring. *A Fierce Heart: Finding Strength, Courage and Wisdom in Any Moment*. Berkeley: Parallax Press, 2017.

Williams, J. Mark G. *The Mindful Way through Depression: Freeing Yourself from Chronic Unhappiness*. Guilford Press, 2007.

ACKNOWLEDGMENTS

This book has been inspired by my personal mindfulness practice, which has been inspired and supported by many individuals and organizations. Above all, I am grateful for Elizabeth. Her encouragement, love, and patience are invaluable to me, as is her personal practice.

As always, I appreciate the support of family. The continual encouragement to grow as a person and teacher has helped me beyond words. Your practice as individuals creates the most beautiful community I could possibly imagine.

I also am grateful for the support of both my teachers and students. This path requires the support of a community, and I am deeply touched to be a part of communities full of such love, kindness, and wisdom.

ABOUT THE AUTHOR

MATTHEW SOCKOLOV is a meditation teacher who currently lives in Playa del Carmen, Mexico. The founding teacher of One Mind Dharma, Matthew leads meditation groups online and works one-on-one with individuals around the world who wish to deepen their practice. He has worked for years with recovering addicts, adolescents, and those who join the community to practice. Empowered as a Buddhist meditation teacher by Spirit Rock Meditation Center, Matthew has worked closely with many teachers in the Theravada Buddhism and Insight Meditation traditions. He has studied with Kevin Griffin, Thānissaro Bhikkhu, and the community at Against the Stream. Matthew lives with his wife, Elizabeth, teaching meditation, spending time outdoors, and enjoying time with his dog and cats. You may find Matthew at mattsock.com. His meditations, free podcast, and writings are available at oneminddharma.com.